2

D0841082

Nathan Hale

Revolutionary Hero

Colonial Leaders

Lord Baltimore *English Politician and Colonist*

Benjamin Banneker *American Mathematician and Astronomer*

William Bradford *Governor of Plymouth Colony*

Benjamin Franklin *American Statesman, Scientist, and Writer*

Anne Hutchinson *Religious Leader*

Cotton Mather *Author, Clergyman, and Scholar*

William Penn *Founder of Democracy*

John Smith *English Explorer and Colonist*

Miles Standish *Plymouth Colony Leader*

Peter Stuyvesant *Dutch Military Leader*

Revolutionary War Leaders

Benedict Arnold *Traitor to the Cause*

Nathan Hale *Revolutionary Hero*

Alexander Hamilton *First U.S. Secretary of the Treasury*

Patrick Henry *American Statesman and Speaker*

Thomas Jefferson *Author of the Declaration of Independence*

John Paul Jones *Father of the U.S. Navy*

Thomas Paine *Political Writer*

Paul Revere *American Patriot*

Betsy Ross *American Patriot*

George Washington *First U.S. President*

Revolutionary

N LINE

Nathan Hale

Revolutionary Hero

Loree Lough

Arthur M. Schlesinger, jr.
Senior Consulting Editor

Chelsea House Publishers

Philadelphia

Produced by 21st Century Publishing and Communications, Inc.
New York, NY. http://www.21cpc.com

CHELSEA HOUSE PUBLISHERS
Editor in Chief Stephen Reginald
Production Manager Pamela Loos
Director of Photography Judy L. Hasday
Art Director Sara Davis
Managing Editor James D. Gallagher

Staff for *NATHAN HALE*
Project Editor/Publishing Coordinator Jim McAvoy
Assistant Editor Anne Hill
Associate Art Director Takeshi Takahashi
Series Design Keith Trego

The Chelsea House World Wide Web address is
http://www.chelseahouse.com

First Printing
1 3 5 7 9 8 6 4 2

Library of Congress Cataloging-in-Publication Data

Lough, Loree.
Nathan Hale / by Loree Lough.
80 pp. cm. — (Revolutionary War Leaders series)
Includes bibliographical references and index.
Summary: Presents a biography of the school teacher turned Revolutionary War soldier who served as an American spy and was captured and eventually executed by the British army.
ISBN 0-7910-5361-X (hc)   ISBN 0-7910-5704-6 (pb)
1. Hale, Nathan, 1755-1776—Juvenile literature. 2. United States—History—Revolution, 1775-1783—Secret service—Juvenile literature. 3. Spies—United States—Biography—Juvenile literature. 4. Soldiers—United States—Biography—Juvenile literature. [1. Hale, Nathan, 1755-1776. 2. Spies. 3. United States—History—Revolution, 1775-1783—Secret service] I. Title. II. Series.
E280.H2L887   1999
973.38'5'092—dc21   99-32043
[B]   CIP

Publisher's Note: In Colonial and Revolutionary War America, there were no standard rules for spelling, punctuation, capitalization, or grammar. Some of the quotations that appear in the Colonial Leaders and Revolutionary War Leaders series come from original documents and letters written during this time in history. Original quotations reflect writing inconsistencies of the period.

Contents

Nathan Hale was born on a prosperous farm nestled in the peaceful countryside of Connecticut. As he grew up, he loved being in the outdoors around the town of Coventry. Enjoying sports made him a strong and athletic young man.

Nathan, the Boy

It was a late spring day. A gentle warm breeze was blowing, and the sweet smell of new grass was in the air. An infant's cry rang out. The newborn was a boy. He was given the name Nathan Hale.

Nathan was born on June 6, 1755 in Coventry, Connecticut. When little Nathan came into the world, Connecticut was not a state but was one of the 13 American **colonies** ruled by Great Britain. With its rolling hills and fertile, green lands, Connecticut was famous for its many farms and abundant crops. It was one of the most prosperous of the colonies. Nathan's parents, Deacon Richard

Hale and Elizabeth Strong Hale, were among the colony's successful farmers.

In colonial times in America, most people had large families. The Hales were no exception. Richard and Elizabeth Hale were the parents of 12 children—nine boys and three girls. Nathan was the sixth child. But the Hales had lost two children as babies, and they were concerned about Nathan.

As a baby, Nathan was sick and weak. He barely survived his first year. Although he improved, he was a pale and thin boy who did not grow as tall and strong as other children his age. His lungs were weak, and he often suffered from nagging coughs. Doctors tried many remedies, and his mother gave him strong, bitter tonics and applied foul-smelling salves to his chest.

But little Nathan refused to let his fragile condition keep him down. His strong spirit and will, as well as the constant care of his parents, helped him overcame his physical weakness. By the time he was a teenager, he had gained weight and grown tall. Nathan loved the outdoors and sports. This also helped him grew stronger. His poor health was finally behind him as he later became an athletic and muscular young man.

When Nathan was growing up, Connecticut and the other 12 American colonies were part of the empire of Great Britain and were ruled by the English king. But Britain was faraway, across the Atlantic Ocean, and colonial Americans were used to a great deal of **self-government**. Connecticut colonists were especially proud of their tradition of ruling themselves. More than 100 years before Nathan was born, the founders of Connecticut had written the first **constitution** that formed a government in America. It was called the Fundamental Orders of Connecticut. This document strongly supported the idea of governments run by their own people.

Nathan's parents also believed that colonists should have the freedom to run their own affairs. Often young Nathan would listen as his father and others talked about the way Britain was treating the colonies. To help pay for running its empire, Britain had placed heavy taxes on many things the colonists had to buy, such as tea, paper, paint, and other goods. In 1765, when Nathan was only 10 years old, Britain passed another new law that forced colonists to pay for supplies for British soldiers in America.

Colonists were angered by a government in London, England, taxing them and forcing them to support British soldiers. By 1769, when young Nathan was ready for college, colonists were already protesting and resisting British laws that denied them their freedoms.

In addition to placing a high value on their freedoms, Nathan's parents were also devout **Puritans**. They strongly believed in leading a moral and ethical life. They also believed in hard work and education, and they expected their children to follow in their footsteps. Many Puritan families hoped that at least one of their

REASONS
W H Y
The *BRITISH* COLONIES,
I N
AMERICA,
SHOULD NOT BE CHARGED WITH
INTERNAL TAXES,
BY AUTHORITY OF
PARLIAMENT;
HUMBLY OFFERED,
For CONSIDERATION,
In Behalf of the Colony of
CONNECTICUT.

NEW - HAVEN;
Printed by B. Mecom. MDCCLXIV.

Nathan could read about Britain's treatment of its colonies in notices like this, published to protest British taxation.

sons would study to become a Puritan minister.

Besides loving the outdoors, Nathan was a good scholar and an avid reader. His father decided the boy should prepare for the ministry. To help Nathan get ready, Richard Hale hired a tutor for his son. The tutor, Reverend Joseph Huntington, thought Nathan was an eager student. By 1769 the teenager was ready to enter Yale College (now Yale University) in the large seaport town of New Haven.

Yale College had been founded by ministers in 1701. It was the third-oldest college in the colonies and had a fine reputation as a place of learning. Nathan was just 14 when he entered Yale College. His 16-year-old brother, Enoch, was also sent to Yale at the same time. In those days, it was not unusual for young men to begin college at such an early age.

Life at Yale was strict, but it was not all studies. Both Nathan and Enoch enjoyed sports. Nathan could kick a ball farther than any other student and he was the champion wrestler at school. He and Enoch also joined a literary society called Linonia. Students in the society discussed topics such as astronomy and literature as well as issues

Nathan studied at Yale College in New Haven and enjoyed many activities. He also talked with fellow students about events that were occurring around him as colonists began to defy British rule over the American colonies.

of the day. They may have also talked about the growing unrest among colonists over the heavy British taxes.

While Nathan was at Yale, colonists, especially in New England, kept up their protests and demonstrations against harsh British rule.

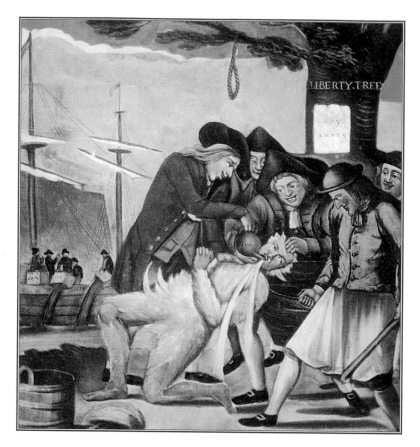

Angry over the tea tax, colonists punish a tax collector by covering him with tar and feathers and pouring tea down his throat.

Crowds in Boston, in the colony of Massachusetts, refused to pay the taxes and attacked tax collectors. Newspapers strongly criticized Britain for its policies, and many New England merchants refused to **import** goods from

Britain rather than pay heavy taxes on them.

Britain's government responded to the colonists' defiance by sending more British troops to Boston. Before long Boston became the center of many of the conflicts. The colonists there resented and hated the British soldiers being in the city. In 1770, the year before Nathan graduated from Yale, several colonists in Boston were killed by British soldiers who fired into a crowd. This event was called the Boston Massacre, and word of it spread quickly throughout the colonies. The colonists became even more bitter about British rule.

One day in March 1770, some boys in Boston began throwing snowballs and sticks at a lone British soldier who was standing guard. The frightened soldier called for help. When other soldiers arrived, they were quickly surrounded by an angry crowd. The two sides began shouting at each other. Suddenly, the soldiers, confused by an officer's command, fired their muskets. When the fighting was over, five Bostonians lay dead. For the first time, blood had been shed in the growing conflict between Britain and its American colonies. This was the Boston Massacre.

In spite of the unrest in the colonies,

Nathan continued his studies. He often took part in college debates, and he helped form a library. He was also appointed a leader in the Linonia Society. Nathan performed in student plays, which delighted the citizens of New Haven. He could often be found enjoying himself at student parties. Nathan was described by his schoolmates and the school officials as "unusually attractive and beloved."

Young Nathan was much respected and admired by other students, by his teachers, and by the townspeople. One citizen of New Haven, Dr. Eneas Munson, described Nathan: "[He was] almost six feet in height, perfectly proportioned, and in figure and [manners] . . . the most manly man I have ever met. . . . [He] was overflowing with good humor, and was the idol of all his acquaintances."

At age 18, Nathan Hale graduated from Yale College with honors. He was among the 13 scholars ranking highest in his class. During the graduation ceremonies, Nathan gave a speech that included an idea unusual for a young man of the time. He talked about the education of women. This was a subject he had often thought about. In colonial times, it was not thought important for most young women to have a higher education. There were no colleges for women, and they could not enter a man's college. If they could read and write, and many could not, it was considered enough. The duties of most women were to take care of their households and children.

In his speech, Nathan spoke about how women's education was not thought to be important. He said, "Whether the education of daughters be not without any just reason, more neglected than that of sons." Many, many years before women could receive higher schooling, Nathan believed girls deserved the same rights to a good education as boys.

When Nathan graduated from Yale College, he began his teaching career in a school like this one. Nathan enjoyed his work, and his pupils and their families admired and respected him for his teaching and his honest and open manner.

2

Nathan, the Schoolteacher

Nathan graduated from Yale in 1773. Rather than becoming a minister, he chose to teach school. He took his first teaching job in East Haddam, a small town in Connecticut. Although Nathan enjoyed teaching immensely, he was not happy with life in the small town. For one thing, he complained that he did not receive enough mail. He also missed the commotion and bustle of New Haven, which was a lively seaport. And he missed the companionship of his college friends too.

His luck soon changed. Only a few months after he began teaching in East Haddam, he was offered a job at Union School in New London, Connecticut. Like New Haven, New London was a busy seaport, with merchant ships constantly sailing in and out of its harbor. New London also had a newspaper, from which Nathan could get news about events in other colonies. And there were town meetings during which citizens could express their ideas about events in New London and in other cities in the colonies.

At Union School, Nathan taught mathematics, Latin, literature, and writing to a class of 30 young men. In 1774, Nathan was also given permission to begin teaching classes to girls. Between the hours of five and seven in the morning, 20 young women filed into Nathan's classroom. It was very early for classes. But the girls would never have been allowed to attend classes during regular school hours. Nathan's friends often joked that the girls were only eager to come to school so early because of Nathan's "good looks" rather than his "good teaching."

While Nathan was teaching in New London,

rumors got started that he was interested in some particular young women. There is no proof, however, that he seriously considered marrying any of them. It is known, though, that two of his college friends used to tease him a lot about having had a crush on his landlord's niece, Elizabeth Adams.

Nathan truly liked teaching. And people in New London liked the amiable young school-teacher. Students, parents, and his employer appreciated Nathan's open and honest manner. He became good friends with many of the town's families and their children, and he kept up his friendships with his college classmates. Then, in late 1774, he was offered the post of master of Union School. After much prayer and soul searching, Nathan accepted the position. It was a happy period for a young man not yet 20 years old.

Nathan would soon find himself taking part in events far outside his schoolroom. The quarrel between the colonists and Britain was heading toward open conflict. Following the Boston Massacre, Britain did back down a bit, and did away with many of the harshest taxes. But the British government was still determined to show the colonists it had final authority over their affairs. Britain kept a tax on tea.

Americans dearly loved to drink their tea. But they had to import it. The heavy tax Britain put on the tea made merchants and other colonists furious. Crowds of angry people held mass meetings in the cities of Boston, Philadelphia, and New York. They were determined to prevent any ships carrying tea from entering their harbors and unloading their cargoes.

In Philadelphia and New York, the citizens peacefully succeeded in keeping the tea ships from landing. It was a different story in Boston. When the English governor of the colony refused to turn back the ships with tea, some colonists took matters into their own hands.

As soon as the ships loaded with tea arrived in Boston Harbor, the Bostonians sent guards to board the ships and make sure none of the tea was unloaded. They asked the captains of the ships to turn around and go back to England with the tea. But the captains could not get permission from the governor to do so. If they sailed back to England without permission, they would be breaking the law, and they would be punished.

So on December 16, 1773, about 5,000 people gathered at the Old South Church to decide what to do. Several dozen **Patriots** put paint on their faces and old blankets around their shoulders to disguise themselves as American Indians. Followed by a huge crowd, they forced their way onto the ships. Some people shouted: "Boston Harbor will be a teapot tonight!" The patriots dumped all the tea overboard into Boston Harbor. They were very careful not to damage anything else.

The next day, John Adams, a leader of the Massachusetts colony, wrote in his dairy: "This destruction of the tea is so bold, so daring, so firm . . . It must have important consequences."

At the Boston Tea Party, crowds on the shore cheered as colonists disguised as American Indians boarded British ships and threw all the tea overboard. The colonists destroyed about $90,000 worth of tea.

Indeed there would be very important consequences. While the colonists were cheering the "Boston Tea Party," the British government was enraged. The colonists had defied British authority and broken British laws. Britain was determined to punish the people of Massachusetts. More soldiers were sent to Boston. More laws were passed denying the Massachusetts colony many of its former rights: Colonists could no longer elect their own local officials such as judges and sheriffs; they could not appoint their own citizens for jury duty; they could not hold their town meetings without permission; and they were forced to allow British soldiers to stay in their homes and eat what little food they had.

News spread quickly throughout the colonies. Nathan soon heard of the Boston Tea Party and Britain's harsh new laws for Massachusetts. He was angry and concerned. He wished he could have been in Boston and part of the action. He also wondered which colonies would be punished next and how they would be able to hold on to their rights. Would there be a war? Would they have to declare independence from Britain? Over the course of the next 18 months, Nathan would discover the answers to these questions.

Leaders set up Committees of Correspondence in towns throughout the colonies so that they could keep in touch with one another and be informed about British actions. This committee meets to discuss events and write letters urging colonists to unite in support of their rights.

3

Nathan, the Soldier

Then, in the fall of 1774, leaders from 12 of the 13 colonies met in Philadelphia, Pennsylvania, for a very important meeting called the **Continental Congress**. This was the first time that the colonies tried to work together for a common cause. The **delegates** took turns speaking. Most of them felt very strongly about the issues. They all knew that something must be done. But they had different opinions about what to do. After many long discussions they finally agreed and issued a formal document. They said in the document that the British laws in the colonies were unjust and the colonists did not have to obey them. They also declared that the royal governors, who were appointed by the king of England to rule each colony, no longer had any authority.

Britain could not allow the colonists to show such defiance and go unpunished. The king immediately sent more troops and warships to the colonies.

By the spring of 1775, people everywhere in the colonies were buzzing with talk of a possible break with Britain. There was even a chance of war. Throughout the colonies, people were kept informed of events by the newly formed **Committees of Correspondence**. In each of the towns, these groups of colonial leaders got together to write letters to one another. The committees informed one another about British activities in their areas. They also wrote statements to be read aloud telling people of their rights. They asked people in the different colonies to work together and support one another. They urged colonists to disagree with

British attempts to take away their rights. Whatever the British did to the people in Boston, the committee in Connecticut, as well as committees in the other colonies, soon knew all about it.

Ordinary people began preparing for war. They started to take action. In Connecticut some Patriots organized a series of "**Tory** hunts." They forced British supporters to change their opinions or leave the colony. In New Hampshire and South Carolina, a few hundred men attacked British forts and stole cannons, guns, and gunpowder. In Virginia and Maryland, Patriots started to form organized armies.

It was in the colony of Massachusetts that the conflict turned into open warfare. In the towns of Lexington and Concord, not far from Boston, a group of armed men from the Massachusetts **militia** exchanged shots with British soldiers. Although the militiamen were outnumbered, they hid behind trees and walls and fired at the lines of marching soldiers. The soldiers' red coats made excellent targets. Caught totally by surprise and unable to withstand the colonists' shots, the soldiers retreated back to Boston. The American Revolution had begun.

In New London 20-year-old Nathan Hale heard the news of the battles. When he attended the town meeting to discuss the events, he rose to express his views. Nathan had a lot of practice giving speeches to his students and was able to inspire people with his passion. He asked the people at the meeting to think about the land they lived on and their farms. He asked if they wanted their land to be governed by outsiders from 3,000 miles away. He called for action, and in a rousing speech urged the people to join in a rebellion against Britain. "Let us march immediately," he said in a stirring voice, "and never lay down our [weapons] until we obtain our independence!"

For Nathan, things had changed forever. His teaching days would soon be behind him. It was time to join in the fight against Britain.

Eager to fight the British, Nathan joined the

In April 1775 the quarrel between America and Britain broke into actual war with the first fight at Concord, Massachusetts. Here, colonial militiamen as well as women and children fight the British as they are retreating from Concord.

Connecticut **regiment**. Armies from around the colonies were marching off to Boston, and men from Nathan's own regiment also left for Massachusetts almost immediately. Nathan had to remain behind, however, until he could fulfill his teaching responsibilities. Although at first

A PLAN of the
TOWN and HARBOUR of
BOSTON.

and the Country adjacent with the
Road from Boston to Concord.
Shewing the Place of the late Engage-
ment between the Kings Troops & the
Provincials, together with the several
Encampments of both Armies in and
about Boston. 19. April 1775.

This map shows the plan of the battles at Lexington and Concord. Marching in close ranks, British soldiers were easy targets for militiamen hiding behind walls and trees.

he was disappointed, he only stayed in New London for a while longer.

By July 1775 Nathan had completed his teaching duties. He had also been given the **commission** of lieutenant in Colonel Charles Webb's 7th Connecticut Regiment. At this point, he was ready to leave for Boston. He gathered his students to tell them the news. The class looked at their teacher with great respect. Nathan prayed with them, shook each one by the hand, and said goodbye.

Nathan also took a little time to return to Yale College for a last visit. While he was there he persuaded several young men to join him in fighting the British. Finally, it was time to leave for Boston and enter into the war for American independence.

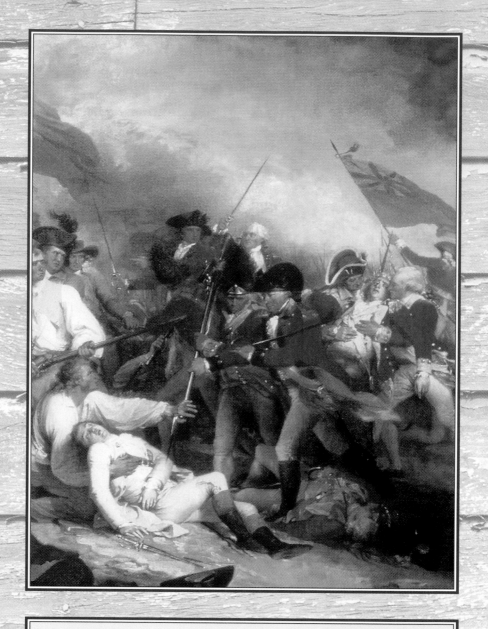

After losing more than 1,000 soldiers, British troops finally overcame colonists at the Battle of Bunker Hill. Although the Americans lost the battle, they surprised the British by showing that they would fight fiercely for their liberty.

4

Nathan,
the Leader

After the battles of Lexington and Concord, the stunned British troops retreated to Boston. There they were immediately surrounded by thousands of angry militiamen. Although Britain sent more warships carrying more troops to Boston, they could not break the **siege** of the city. British soldiers were trapped inside Boston, and their food and supplies were cut off.

The British sent three of their most experienced generals to Boston to try to break the siege. They planned an attack on rebel forts around the city. They also planned to take supplies and ammunition that the colonists were storing in the town of Cambridge. The Patriots learned of the enemy's plans and decided to act before the British could move. If they could put cannons on the heights north of Boston, they could fire down on the British ships in the harbor.

On the night of June 16, 1775, militiamen led by Colonel Israel Putnam of Connecticut, traveling quickly and quietly, reached the heights of Charlestown across the river from Boston. There were two hills on the heights, Bunker Hill and Breed's Hill. All through the night the men dug trenches and built sturdy walls of earth and wooden logs around both hills to protect them in the coming battle. Breed's Hill was the lowest hill and closer to Boston, so the militiamen built the strongest fortifications there.

When the sun came up, the British were astounded to see fortifications on the two hills. British warships were given the order and immediately began to bombard the forts.

Great barges carrying large groups of British soldiers began crossing the river with orders to attack. Behind the forts, the militiamen waited.

Marching in long, straight lines, British soldiers moved up Breed's Hill. As they got closer, Colonel Putnam rode his horse along the Patriot line, shouting out loudly to the Americans, "Don't shoot until you see the whites of their eyes!" At the right moment, when the militiamen did fire, scores of British soldiers instantly fell dead or wounded.

The British had fully expected that the Americans would panic and run. Instead, it was the British soldiers who retreated back down the hill. Reinforcements arrived, and once more the British soldiers marched up the hill. Again, the huge volley of shots from the Americans immediately cut them down. On the third attempt, however, the British soldiers finally captured Breed's Hill. Not long thereafter they also captured Bunker Hill. By then the brave Patriots were greatly outnumbered and nearly out of ammunition, so they retreated.

The Battle of Bunker Hill was a costly victory for the British. They lost more than 1,000 officers and soldiers. Even though in the end the Americans did not win the battle, they had showed that they could fight, and the battle inspired more and more colonists to join the rebellion. In time, Americans started to think of Bunker Hill as a victory after all, only a different kind of victory. As one Patriot said: "I wish we could sell them another hill at the same price."

Benjamin Franklin was an important colonial leader. After hearing the terrible news about the Battle of Bunker Hill, he wrote this letter to one of the British lawmakers:

You are a member of Parliament and one of that majority which has doomed my country to destruction. You have begun to burn our towns and murder our people. Look upon your hands! They are stained with the blood of your relations! You and I were long friends. You are now my enemy and I am

Yours,

B Franklin

Nathan could hardly wait to get to Boston and join the fight. Still, he did not get there until January 1776. By that time, General George Washington had arrived outside Boston. Washington had been appointed commander of the new Continental Army. He had to organize the thousands of volunteers who were streaming into Massachusetts. Then he had to train them and turn them into fighting soldiers. But first, he had to try to end the siege of Boston, which had been dragging on for months.

When Nathan finally arrived in Boston, he was given a commission as a captain in the newly formed 19th Continental Regiment. For Nathan, everything around him was exciting. He kept a diary, in which he recorded even the most boring activities of a young officer on the front lines of battle. Nathan did not think camp life was dull. He quietly admitted to his friends that he would not have taken a leave of absence, even if it had been offered.

Nathan's diary entries showed that he thoroughly enjoyed every aspect of military life.

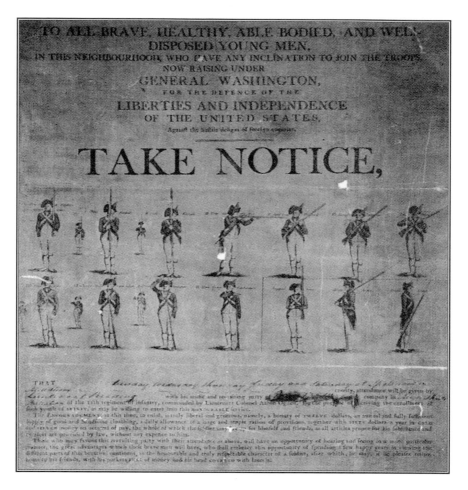

George Washington needed a great many soldiers in order to defeat the British. This "Take Notice" poster urges young men to join the Continental Army and fight for independence.

He gladly took on the duties of a company commander. He worried about his men and their well-being, even when they complained about their superior officers. Sometimes Nathan complained about his superiors too.

Just as he had wanted to be a good teacher, Nathan also wanted to be a very good leader. He quickly earned the respect of the men under his command. Once, some of his men who had become very weary of a soldier's life wanted to quit and go home. Nathan offered to divide his salary among them if they would stay in the army a while longer.

Nathan tried to see that his men had proper uniforms and were housed as well as possible in the camp around Boston. If they became ill, he could

George Washington did not have an easy task getting willing soldiers for the Continental Army. Many were militiamen from the various colonies who volunteered. They left their homes and signed up to serve for only a few months. When their time was up, they wanted to get back to their homes and families. Soldiers who were farmers were particularly anxious to return to their farms when it was time to plant their crops or harvest them. It took a great deal of persuasion by many passionate officers just like Nathan to convince enough able men to stay and fight for independence.

often be found beside them, praying and talking with them.

One day Nathan received a letter from one of his friends. Nathan was moved by what he read in the letter. His friend told him about a pamphlet called *Common Sense*. It was written by Thomas Paine, a writer and Patriot who lived in Philadelphia, Pennsylvania. Paine helped rouse the colonists to action when he first wrote that they should break away from Britain and become free. In plain and simple language he said Britain had nothing to offer Americans and that Americans had the right to their own government and their own laws. He gave many compelling reasons why America's independence from Britain was the right and natural thing.

The pamphlet sold for one penny, and thousands of people bought it. Teachers read it to their pupils and General Washington had it read aloud to the soldiers in the Continental Army. Paine's words in the pamphlet *Common Sense*

For most Americans, uniforms like these of the soldier (left) and the officer (right) were often scarce.

made many colonists decide that they wanted their freedom and independence from Britain and that it was worth fighting for.

The pamphlet had also made a great impact on Nathan's friend. His friend wrote that the "little pamphlet" had helped him make up his mind. He, and many others just like him, were so inspired that they joined the army and took up arms.

In the meantime, in the the harsh winter of 1775–76, General Washington was preparing the army to fight. He kept the troops around Boston busy drilling and learning how to be good soldiers. He knew that the siege of Boston would not finally be over until he could drive all of the British out. But he needed cannons to be able to do that. When cannons and ammunition finally did arrive, Washington planned a bold attack and quickly seized the heights south of Boston. His men built strong forts and then mounted the cannons there. Washington gave specific instructions that the cannons were to be pointed at the British warships, which were still in Boston Harbor.

Without their powerful ships, the British

British soldiers drill and march in ranks near Boston. Patriot volunteers also had to drill and learn to march as General George Washington began to organize and train the Continental Army and end the siege of Boston.

would be completely lost in the war. When the British general saw Washington's cannons aimed at his ships, he hastily marched his army

Once the British left Boston, General Washington had to decide where he would move his troops next. Here he looks over maps and discusses plans with his officers.

out of Boston and onboard the ships. The British sailed away without a fight. To the Americans' surprise they had won a major victory over the British and saved the city of

Boston at the same time.

But Washington knew that the fighting was far from over. The British were not going to give up so easily. They would be back and in greater numbers. He believed that the colony of New York would very likely be the next place the British would attack. In the spring of 1776 General Washington directed the Connecticut regiment of the army to move to New York to defend the city. Nathan marched with his regiment to New London, Connecticut, and then sailed to New York from there.

Once in New York, Nathan's duties included keeping records, organizing supplies, and supervising guard duty. But he was anxious to see action. He soon did. In July 1776 the same general who had earlier fled from Boston landed on Long Island, New York. He had 30,000 British soldiers with him and orders to capture New York City. His assignment was to break the rebellious colonists' spirits and end the revolution.

Washington quickly marched his army from Boston to New York to try to protect the city. Once on Long Island, Washington's soldiers began building strong fortifications. With 10,000 men under his command, he prepared for the battle to come. First the British attacked Brooklyn Heights on Long Island, and the out-numbered Americans were quickly defeated. When Washington ordered a hasty retreat to Manhattan Island, Nathan and his regiment were with him. Luckily for the Americans the British did not follow up their victory with another attack right away.

Nathan found himself stationed along the banks of the East River in New York City. Eager to see more action, he planned a risky mission. With a few members of his regiment, he rowed out into the East River where a British supply ship was anchored. The ship was guarded by a warship with many heavy guns. If Nathan could capture the British supply ship, he would have much-needed supplies for the American fighting men. Amazingly, with the element of surprise on their side, Nathan and his small group of men succeeded in capturing the crew of the supply ship. Then they towed the ship, with all of its goods and ammunition, to the shore.

His boldness and daring earned Nathan respect as a leader of fighting men. His courage also brought him to the attention of Colonel Thomas Knowlton, who had formed a band of men called Knowlton's Rangers. The Rangers had been ordered by Washington to patrol the shorelines along Manhattan Island. When Knowlton needed another officer to assist him, he chose Nathan to be a company commander in the Rangers.

The British soldiers still held Long Island, and General Washington knew they would soon attack Manhattan. He desperately needed information about when and where the attack would happen. "We have not been able to obtain the least information as to the enemy's plans," he wrote on September 6. The general asked Colonel Knowlton to find him a volunteer from the Rangers. Washington needed a spy to sneak behind the British lines and gather the information he desperately needed.

When Knowlton approached several men, he was met with dead silence at first. Then one man spoke. He said, "I am willing to be shot, but I am not willing to be hanged." (Spies who were caught would be hanged.) Then, a quiet voice broke the stillness. The speaker, still pale and weak from a recent illness, rose slowly to his feet. Knowlton immediately recognized the man as his youngest captain. Nathan knew at once that this might be his only opportunity to serve his country and do his duty. "I will undertake the mission," he said.

Later that same day Nathan's best friend, Captain William Hull, tried desperately to talk him out of becoming a spy. Hull reminded Nathan that spying was extremely dangerous. He also said that Nathan's nature was "too frank and open for deceit and disguise." And finally, he told Nathan that no one really respects a spy anyway. Nathan argued that spying *was* in fact an honorable activity. Information he might gain could possibly help the Americans win the war against the British. Nathan said "I wish to be useful, and every kind of service necessary to the public good becomes honorable by being necessary."

These were the very last recorded words ever spoken by Nathan Hale until the final speech he made only moments before his untimely death. His good friend William Hull never heard from Nathan again.

During the war, General George Washington put Benjamin Tallmadge, a close friend and Yale classmate of Nathan's, in charge of spying on the British. Tallmadge had a network of spies including merchants, farmers, tailors, and women. Lydia Darragh of Philadelphia was one of them. Lydia overheard a British conversation. Her husband wrote the information on scraps of paper. Then Lydia hid the scraps in buttons on her son's coat. The boy slipped past soldiers to meet his brother, an officer in the American army. The boy ripped off the buttons, and General Washington received the critical messages.

British warships entering the waters around New York City. The ships sailed into the East River and unloaded great numbers of soldiers onto the island of Manhattan. Overwhelmed by the British forces the Continental Army was driven northward.

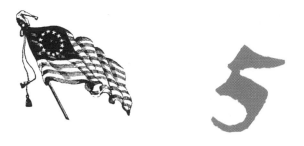

Nathan,
the Spy

Captain Nathan Hale started out on his top-secret assignment on September 12, 1776. The American army he left behind had moved to the northern part of Manhattan Island and was camped on a place called Harlem Heights overlooking the Hudson River. It was important that Nathan get to Long Island to find out what he could about British plans to attack Manhattan.

Nathan left his uniform and a few other personal belongings behind. He planned to pass himself off as a Dutch schoolteacher. To prove his role, he took his diploma from Yale College with him. Other than pretending to be a schoolteacher looking for work, Nathan was not well prepared to spy. Captain Knowlton did not give him any specific things to look and listen for. And Nathan had no code to use if he wrote messages. At the time invisible ink existed, but Nathan did not carry any with him.

Because British warships prevented him from crossing the East River, he went north from Harlem Heights to Norwalk, Connecticut. There he took a boat to Long Island and landed near Huntington. Before entering the British area, he instructed the boatman to come back in a few days to pick him up. He then spent some days going through British army camps on Long Island. Nathan watched and listened for any information. He drew maps and made notes.

On the appointed day, at the appointed time, Nathan returned to the boat landing, ready to go, and signaled a boat from the shore. He was pleased with himself. He felt he had gotten information that would help General Washington.

Something was wrong, however. Suddenly Nathan realized that the boat was not the same one he had taken before. It was a British **frigate.** Quickly, he tried to retrace his steps back over the cold muddy ground and deeper into the woods. If the British caught him, Nathan knew he would be doomed.

What he did not know then was that the British had already captured New York City. On September 14 a group of British ships had appeared in the East River near a place called Kips Bay. Units of militiamen were stationed along the river, and they watched as the ships loaded their cannons. The leaders of the militia did not seem to know what to do. When the men heard the cannons fire and saw British troops marching ashore, they ran.

As the retreating Americans headed north on Manhattan Island, they came upon General Washington with a group of Connecticut officers. They tried to rally the fleeing militia- men as Washington shouted at them to stand

and fight. But it was no use. The militiamen paid no attention to the officers and just kept on running. Most of Manhattan Island was lost to the British.

When Nathan realized that the British had probably taken the city, he decided to cross over into Manhattan. It seemed as if the information he had now would be useless. Still, he wanted to find out more. He got into New York City and began making notes on the number of British troops and their forts.

In the meantime, General Washington was in northern Manhattan at Harlem Heights with his army. As Washington watched from the Heights, a group of Connecticut Rangers led by Nathan's commander, Colonel Thomas Knowlton, fought a **skirmish** with groups of British soldiers who had already marched north. As Knowlton and his Rangers held off the British soldiers, more Patriot volunteers from the area rushed in to help.

The Americans and British fought back and

forth in what was then a wheat field. The British soldiers finally ran out of ammunition and retreated. The Americans followed, yelling and shooting. This Battle of Harlem Heights was a small victory for the Americans. Sadly, however, they lost Colonel Knowlton, who was killed in the action.

General Washington soon realized that the British wanted to make New York City their headquarters. So he decided to burn it instead. On September 20 he sent men to set the city on fire. From Harlem Heights, Washington watched as flames rose in the night sky. A strong wind carried the fire from building to building. By the time the British could put out the fires, more than a quarter of the city was burned to the ground.

Before the fire began, Nathan had wandered through the city taking more notes on British movements. No one knows for sure, but it is thought that he had helped set the city on fire. Angered by the fire, the British began checking

Fire rages in New York City in September 1776. General Washington ordered his men to set the city ablaze so that the British would not be able to use it as their winter quarters.

the identities of all of the young American men they found in the city. They jailed more than 200 men whom they suspected of setting the blaze. Thousands of angry British soldiers roamed the streets. They accused anyone they did not recognize of being a spy and an enemy.

Nathan could not escape the many soldiers. He was caught on the night of September 21. When the soldiers searched him, they found the notes he had hidden in his shoes. He was accused of spying and was taken in chains to the headquarters of General William Howe, the British commander in New York. It was later claimed by Nathan's father that Nathan was betrayed by his cousin, Samuel Hale, who was a Tory. Samuel was in New York serving the British army as the person in charge of American prisoners at the time Nathan was captured.

The papers found on Nathan marked him a spy. Still, he gave General Howe the story he had planned earlier in case he got caught. He was a schoolteacher, he explained, hoping to find a job in New York. Howe did not believe a word of it. The diploma seemed legitimate enough, but how could Nathan explain the other, more suspicious papers that were found in his shoes?

General William Howe was commander of the British troops in New York City. When Nathan, a captured spy, refused to sign a pledge of loyalty to Britain, Howe ordered him to be hanged.

Howe insisted that Nathan confess immediately. And confess he did. Nathan willingly and proudly admitted he was an officer in the Continental Army and gave the reason for his mission. Certainly, thought Nathan, General Howe would respect an honest soldier doing his duty.

General Howe's chief engineer and aide, John Montresor, later claimed that the general was indeed moved by Nathan's patriotism. Despite this, Nathan was forced onto the seat of a hard wooden chair and ordered to sign a pledge of loyalty to the English king. General Howe made it clear that deserters, spies, and other criminals were whipped, shot, or hanged. If Nathan signed the pledge, his life would be spared, but at what cost?

With courage and dignity, Nathan went to his death on September 22, 1776. His final words became an inspiration to thousands of Americans fighting for freedom.

Nathan, the Hero

Nathan knew very well the price he would pay for refusing to sign the pledge. He believed, however, that his life was a small price to pay in comparison to giving up his freedom and betraying his general. He would die, if need be, to show his loyalty and **allegiance** to his brand-new nation. Nathan knew that the colonies had declared their independence from Britain.

While he had been stationed in New York City with his regiment, colonial leaders had met in Philadelphia and decided that it was time to be a nation completely independent from Britain. At the meeting they drew up a document that separated them forever from Britain. It was the Declaration of Independence. Many men from different colonies contributed their thoughts and ideas, but it was Thomas Jefferson, a young lawyer from Virginia, who wrote the document. In the Declaration, Jefferson wrote that all men are created equal and have the right to "Life, Liberty, and the pursuit of Happiness." He also wrote that citizens had a right to **revolt** against any government that treated them unjustly. He said that they could and should form their own government. On July 4, 1776, the colonial leaders who met in Philadelphia signed the document and sent the news throughout the colonies. On this day the United States of America was born.

Nathan continued to refuse to sign a pledge of loyalty to the king, and Howe ordered that he be hanged. Howe was so angry that he did not even allow Nathan to have a trial. As a soldier, he would have been entitled to a military trial called a court-martial. But Nathan had not

**American citizens gather and rejoice in
the town square as they hear a reading
of the Declaration of Independence.**

been dressed as a soldier and could not prove
he was in the Continental Army. And he had
confessed to being a spy.

Nathan was held overnight under guard at

General Howe's headquarters. He asked for writing materials, which Montresor gave him. The engineer had taken pity on the courageous young man. Nathan spent the night writing a letter to his brother Enoch and to Colonel Knowlton. He did not know that Knowlton had been killed at Harlem Heights.

British officer Major William Cunningham was in charge of Nathan's execution. He was a mean-spirited man and refused to see that the letters were delivered. Cunningham, who was noted for his cruelty, said that he did not want the "rebels" to know that Nathan was a man "who could die with so much firmness."

On Sunday, September 22, 1776, at 11 o'clock in the morning, Cunningham, Montresor, and some soldiers marched Nathan to an apple orchard north of Howe's headquarters. Nathan had asked for a Bible and a minister, but Cunningham would not allow it. Before they placed the noose around Nathan's neck, he had a few words with Montresor. Montresor was greatly moved at what he later recalled as the "gentle dignity, the consciousness of [rightness] and high intentions" of Nathan's last moments.

Calm and proud, Nathan accepted his fate. When asked if he had any last words before the noose tightened around his neck, he spoke about American liberty and prayed for freedom for his countrymen. "You are shedding the blood of the innocent," he declared. "If I had ten thousand lives, I would lay them all down in defense of my injured bleeding country." Then Nathan uttered his famous words: "I only regret that I have but one life to lose for my country."

When Nathan spoke his last words, he may have been thinking of a play called *Cato*, which he surely knew. Written by a 17th-century English poet, Joseph Addison, it was the story of an early Roman statesman named Cato. Cato was totally honest and upright and devoted to the ideas of liberty. He gave his life for Rome rather than give in to a tyrant. Nathan used Cato's words in the play as he, an 18th-century American hero, went to his death.

Nathan's body was left hanging from the

apple tree beside the road for many days. Eventually, British soldiers took down Nathan's body and buried him in an unmarked grave. He was only 21 years old.

British General Howe must have hoped that the sight of Nathan's body would be a lesson to other Americans not to side with the Patriots. In all likelihood, however, Nathan's death served the opposite purpose. Captain Nathan Hale had been a brave patriot. His imprisonment and hanging only proved that he had great courage and an unstoppable spirit. Rather than discouraging other colonists from joining the American cause, Nathan's fate encouraged other Americans to continue their struggle and fight for freedom.

When Nathan's friend, William Hull, learned about Nathan's death, he asked to enter the British camp under a white flag of truce. There he sought out Montresor. The engineer told Hull that Cunningham had showed Nathan's letters and Yale diploma to Major John Wyllys, a prisoner of war who was also a close friend and classmate of Nathan's. Later, Hull added the information he gathered from Montresor to his memoirs. It is very likely that Hull's report was the source of a story that later appeared in a newspaper article about Nathan Hale's last moments of life.

Hull relayed the details of Nathan's last hours to Nathan's brother Enoch. Although seven of Nathan's brothers served in the army, Nathan was the only one to die in the American Revolution. Enoch rode from the Hale home in Coventry to General Washington's new camp at White Plains, New York. He wanted, he said, "to learn the truth and talk some of my brother" with Nathan's fellow officers.

After learning what he could about Nathan's death, Enoch sorted through his brother's belongings. Among them he found Nathan's diary. Today, people can see several of the items Enoch found, along with paintings and sculptures, at the Hale homestead in Coventry.

Nathan Hale is commemorated with this statue in New York City, where he gave his life for his country.

Soon after Nathan's death, one of his teachers at Yale composed a poem in honor of the young hero. In 1812, a fort at the entrance to the harbor of New Haven was named for Nathan

Hale. He was also commemorated with a large granite memorial in Coventry. A bronze statue of Nathan also stands near Connecticut's capitol building in Hartford. And many more statues have been erected and streets named in honor of Nathan.

Then, more than 200 years after his death, on October 1, 1985, Connecticut honored Nathan Hale by making him the state's official hero. "By every action of his short life," wrote a member of a landmarks society, "Nathan Hale exemplified the ideals of patriotism." Another writer perhaps summed up Nathan's short life best when he wrote: "If Nathan Hale's **deeds** did not qualify him as a hero, his choices certainly did, for the heroism *is* the choice."

GLOSSARY

allegiance–loyalty to one's country, government, or ruler

colony–a place where people live but are ruled by the laws of a faraway country

commission–the rank given to a military officer

Committees of Correspondence–groups of men who wrote letters to one another giving information about events during the American Revolution

constitution–a document that gives a set of principles for governing

Continental Congress–the group of colonial leaders who gathered to discuss the conflict between America and Britain.

deed–something that is done; action

delegate–a person who represents others

frigate–a fast, three-masted warship

import–to bring in goods from another country

militia–a group of men who are called to serve in the military in emergencies

Patriots–people who believed America should be a country separate from Britain

Puritan–a person who is very strict in religion and morals

regiment–a unit in an army

revolt–an uprising by a group of people against authority

self-government–government organized and run by the people

siege–the surrounding of a military place by an army to force surrender

skirmish–a small fight that does not become a major battle

Tory–a person who remained loyal to Britain during the American Revolution

CHRONOLOGY

1755 Born on June 6 in Coventry, Connecticut.

1769 Enters Yale College in New Haven with brother Enoch.

1773 Graduates from Yale College with honors; accepts a teaching position in East Haddam, Connecticut; moves to New London, Connecticut to teach at Union School.

1774 Granted permission to teach young women.

1775 Joins the Connecticut regiment; accepts a commission as lieutenant in Colonel Charles Webb's 7th Connecticut Regiment.

1776 Promoted to captain in the newly formed Continental Army; sent to New York City with the army; joins Colonel Thomas Knowlton's Rangers; volunteers to spy behind British lines in New York for General George Washington; captured by the British on September 21; hanged the following day as a spy.

REVOLUTIONARY WAR TIME LINE

1765   The Stamp Act is passed by the British. Violent protests against it break out in the colonies.

1766   Britain ends the Stamp Act.

1767   Britain passes a law that taxes glass, painter's lead, paper, and tea in the colonies.

1770   Five colonists are killed by British soldiers in the Boston Massacre.

1773   People are angry about the taxes on tea. They throw boxes of tea from ships in Boston harbor into the water. It ruins the tea. The event is called the Boston Tea Party.

1774   The British pass laws to punish Boston for the Boston Tea Party. They close Boston harbor. Leaders in the colonies meet to plan a response to these actions.

1775   The battles of Lexington and Concord begin the American Revolution.

1776   The Declaration of Independence is signed. France and Spain give money to help the Americans fight Britain. Nathan Hale is captured by the British. He is charged with being a spy and is executed.

1777   Leaders choose a flag for America. The American troops win some important battles over the British. General Washington and his troops spend a very cold, hungry winter in Valley Forge.

1778 France sends ships to help the Americans win the war. The British are forced to leave Philadelphia.

1779 French ships head back to France. The French support the Americans in other ways.

1780 Americans discover that Benedict Arnold is a traitor. He escapes to the British. Major battles take place in North and South Carolina.

1781 The British surrender at Yorktown.

1783 A peace treaty is signed in France. British troops leave New York.

1787 The U.S. Constitution is written. Delaware becomes the first state in the Union.

1789 George Washington becomes the first president. John Adams is vice president.

FURTHER READING

Ford, David S. *The Interrogation of Nathan Hale.* Woodstock, IL: The Dramatic Press, 1997.

Hagman, Harlan L. *Nathan Hale.* Detroit, MI: Heart of the Lakes Press, 1992.

Hale, Reverend Edward Everett. *A Biography of Captain Nathan Hale.* Hartford, CN: Society of the Sons of the American Revolution, 1998.

Monjo, F.N. *A Namesake for Nathan.* New York: Coward, McCann & Geoghegan, 1977.

Seymour, George Dudley. *Hale: Documentary Life of Nathan Hale.* Salem, MA: Higginson Press, 1995.

INDEX